CW00819354

WE, THE HEARTBROKEN

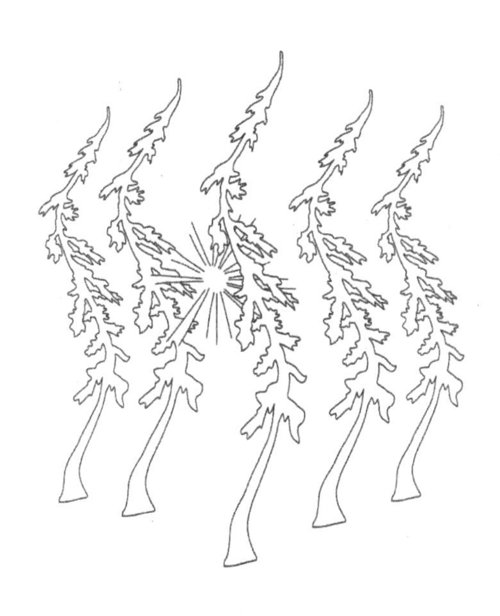

First published in the United Kingdom in 2023
by Hajar Press C.I.C.
www.hajarpress.com
@hajarpress

ISBN 978-1-914221-16-3 Paperback
ISBN 978-1-914221-17-0 EPUB eBook

A Cataloguing-in-Publication data record for this book is available from the British Library.

'We, the Heartbroken (Outro)' was first published on the Pluto Press website on 3 December 2020. Used by permission.
www.plutobooks.com/blog/we-the-heartbroken

Cover and interior art: Han Gunji Stephens
Cover design: Samara Jundi
Typesetting: Laura Jones / lauraflojo.com

Printed and bound in the United Kingdom by
Clays Ltd, Elcograf S.p.A.

WE, THE HEARTBROKEN

GARGI BHATTACHARYYA

For my family by blood, imagination or laughter.

If ever any one of you found yourself beside a fidgety older brown person, sharing a wink or a giggle or a yawn. Maybe blocking the street or bringing down the fences. Maybe holding the banner or the placard or the leaflets. Quite often in search of a toilet. Or a snack. Or just an escape from the speeches. Please know that every fleeting instance of human contact buoyed up my spirit and brought me just enough joy to take the next step.

I hope I did the same for you.

Contents

PLAYLIST

Nina Simone – 'Everything Must Change'

Chet Baker – 'September Song'

Roy Bailey – 'The World Turned Upside Down'

Judy Garland – 'Just in Time – Live at the London Palladium/1964'

Stevie Wonder – 'For Once in My Life'

The Source feat. Candi Staton – 'You Got the Love'

The Pogues – 'If I Should Fall from Grace with God'

Barbara Lewis – 'Hello Stranger'

Sarah Vaughan – 'Speak Low – Live at the London House, Chicago/1958'

Billy Bragg – 'Waiting for the Great Leap Forwards'

Louis Armstrong – 'La vie en rose'

WE, THE HEARTBROKEN (INTRO)

Heartbreak is an elastic kind of pain. Maybe the loss of a family, the devastation of a community, the displacement of a whole people. But also, perhaps, the loss of a lover. The humiliation of dashed hopes. The imprecise sense of unease that can swirl around a life, stealing joy no matter what you do.

But mention heartbrokenness and others turn to pay attention, opening their own hurts to meet yours. Commonality in sorrow seeps out when so many other commonalities never land. Joy? That is all too often something limited. Perhaps we're too enthralled in the sensation, perhaps quietly anxious that elation cannot be shared too widely. Worried that, unlike grief, there is never quite enough joy to go around.

Looking back over this book, I find I seem to have turned heartbrokenness into grief. And there is so much already said about grief. Meditations and self-help guides, routes to therapy and routes to oblivion. I did not set out to write about grief and grieving, although it can never be said too often to be kind to yourselves.

So this is not really a book about 'grief', despite my own confusion about what is grief and what is heartbrokenness. It is—is trying to be—a book about how the experience and anticipation of grief sit within and alongside a registering of collective sorrow—and how there can be no remaking of the world without ways to allow for our collective sorrow.

Heartbrokenness is aligned to grief. I admit that. When I speak of our collective heartbreak, grief must be in the mix, as it is in every reckoning with human lives considered in the round.

But *We, the Heartbroken* is not only a description of living with mortality, although that is also part of it. We are the broken-hearted not only because of loss, but also because of knowledge. Not only because life ends, but also because life disappoints. And, most of all, not only because into each life some rain must fall, but also because the deluge washing away the possibilities of human life sweeps down generations, reducing us all.

In my annoying way—*get off, get off, can't you see we are hurting*—I want to persuade you that grief is a necessary component of a revolutionary imagination. This means that grief cannot be tucked away or managed, because without the consciousness of grief, we cannot remain open to each other and to the implications and possibilities of our profound interdependence. Address grief as a personal wound, something to make us stronger, an opportunity to display that most dubious of attributes, resilience, and the tiny cracks through which collective redemption might seep begin to close up. Wear your personal grief as a badge of honour or celebrated battle-wound, and suddenly grieving also becomes a contest.

Heartbreak is the unhappy knowledge that there is nothing special, nothing special at all, about our individual grief. But it is also an understanding that none of us have anything to prove. If we are not yet in a state of sorrow ... well, this is no more than chance. Sorrow is on its way. It is in the lives before us and around us. Heartbreak is a better word for what it feels like when we grasp that every sorrow is repeated, amplified, transposed. When I speak of our heartbrokenness, I am trying to capture this sorrow that moves between individual grief and the consciousness of all that is so broken in our world.

Grief unsettles in a way that moves between the private life and the collective horror. And the unsettlement moves in both directions. Personal loss can open you to the whole overwhelming ocean of human loss, while an appreciation, however analytic, of the waste of life through the ages can niggle away as a constant reminder of your own inescapable mortality. So, although this book is not a guide to managing any private grief, it does take the language of grief and re-use it as a way to think about sorrow as an unavoidable and probably necessary component of any seriously transformative politics.

Human broken-heartedness longs for two things: ways to feel better and ways of believing that our pain is meaningful. In reality, both are hard asks.

Towards the end of her life, Elisabeth Kübler-Ross wrote that she was unnerved by the popular take-up of her schematisation of the stages of grief, not least by the rush to use the schema as a way of tidying away all the messiness.[1] At its worst, the Kübler-Ross model turns grieving into a self-improvement programme. *Complete each stage as specified to become a fully accredited survivor of grief.* Kübler-Ross herself was adamant that the stages were not challenges to be overcome, and the model certainly not a training manual for those seeking to build up their emotional muscle.

In fact, *On Death and Dying*, in which Kübler-Ross first outlines the stages of grief, is about those dying as opposed to those left behind.[2] The grief, then, is the grief arising from imagining the life we have lost, the life we will never live. The psychic journey of those diagnosed with a terminal illness is headlined with the now famous five stages: Denial, Anger, Bargaining, Depression, Acceptance. An expanded version of her model includes two other stages, Shock and Testing, signalling further complexity. The terrible aptness of this schema,

1 Elisabeth Kübler-Ross and David Kessler, *On Grief and Grieving: Finding the Meaning of Grief Through the Five Stages of Loss*, New York: Simon & Schuster, 2005.

2 Elisabeth Kübler-Ross, *On Death and Dying: What the Dying Have to Teach Doctors, Nurses, Clergy and Their Own Families*, New York: Macmillan, 1969.

somehow speaking to so many, seeming to put into words what they already felt, ends up leading to a kitschy ubiquity. What was a serious clinical and scholarly attempt to comprehend human heartbreak has become the stuff of self-help tea towels. We laugh about denial while longing for acceptance. But the repetition should not make the steps useless. Perhaps the familiarity adds comfort. A sort of secular mantra, a road map for how we might treat each other.

David Kessler, one of Kübler-Ross' collaborators, later added a final stage: Meaning. This is a stage beyond Acceptance, indicating arrival at a point where the experience of loss makes sense, perhaps even reframes our attitude to life and to others. I have not included a stage called Meaning in this book. I understand the wish to round things off so that it all seems to make sense and to serve a purpose. Everyone wants to think that what we suffer is somehow meaningful. But while I believe that every life has meaning, it is dangerous to think of the heartbreak of living in our broken world as translatable into the comfort of meaning. We are heartbroken not because the cumulative losses of our lives and others' give sense to some overall order. We are heartbroken because it is all so meaningless.

One lesson of this work, then, is to try to stop making heartbrokenness into an occasion for meaning-making.

Kübler-Ross herself championed the value of understanding grief, not seeking to fix it. So the stages are not a programme. We cannot force our way through them more quickly to gain our certificates in successful grieving. Instead, they are a shorthand through which to understand the apparently random and often distressing behaviour of those lost in grief.

The sections of this book repurpose the Kübler-Ross stages because of their familiarity. Every heading can and should be stretched, as their creator suggested. Having been ejected from medical training into the free-floating realms of management theory and self-help, the Kübler-Ross model has been a bit down on its luck. Now referencing the stages of grief makes it sound as if you know nothing about the complexities of human emotion at all. But few other scholarly frameworks have had such a reach into the ways we comprehend and talk about difficult emotions in everyday life. And whatever their limitations or unintended applications, people really believe that these stages correspond with how they feel.

So, although what follows is a kind of unfunny joke—*ha ha ha, look at this trite attempt to narrate the most momentous human emotions*—it is also a nod to a democratised language of understanding. Rehabilitating pop psychology as part of the soundtrack of our lives, a counterpart to pop music and throwaway telly, makes space for the collaged fragments through which we tell our lives back to ourselves. Because that magpie-will to gather up the remains of a commodified existence and make something of our human life and its loves endure—that, too, is a kind of everyday intellectualism.

I don't believe we can build a different, better world without being heartbroken.

When we try to tidy up, squash down and split off our heartbreak from all the other heartbreaks, we endanger our sense that *this cannot go on*.

Please don't think that I am celebrating breakdown. We all need to keep living, however we can, among the debris of the now, even as we hallucinate flashes of the future. But there is no dream of other tomorrows without some heartbreak today.

Managing heartbreak can seem like a turning inwards and away from the world. The guides to surviving (or letting go or uncovering your secret self or thriving or just keeping calm and carrying on) centre the self. Sometimes they point to service to others, it is true, but in the main they address a lonely predicament.

But heartbreak is also what can open us to each other, washing us up in the seas of human sufferings, large and small.

Not quite an identification, with all its implications of a demarcated self matching itself with suitably similar others (with the accompanying message, of course, that there are others who remain unmatched), but a disidentification with the self. Heartbreak is also a kind of reverie, a cutting free from what anchors us in the mundane. So, maybe no washing up, but equally, perhaps, no self-consciousness.

We speak very often of class consciousness as a mode of collective self-knowledge. Of course, this is what revolutionary promise has relied on: the class agents will come to consciousness in a manner that forces action. That it is the monster rising. Perhaps we are sleeping now, the fitful sleep of discomfort, but when our dreams chime together, we will awake. And then? Well, then the world will see.

I, too, am in love with this heroic narrative, immersed in the worldview it implies, charting my actions and relations to others always in anticipation of this revelation to come. But it makes a difference how we imagine this story. Perhaps we think of struggle as a battle scene, appropriately glamourised, with a crescendo of inspirational and choreographed unity, perhaps akin to the flying slow-motion high kicks of the martial arts movies but with an ocean of perfectly extended legs filling the screen and our consciousness as a new tomorrow is born ...

But what comes before the high kicks of revolutionary badassness includes sadness.

Perhaps sadness is the most important step. The thing that makes it possible for us to see each other and the world and what has been and is being done to us all.

SHOCK

The warning is as much for others as for the grief-stricken. And this has been such an important popularised insight. Now there is a widespread understanding that the jolt of grief can be somatised, setting off our physiological responses to extreme stress or danger. Trying to catch someone in this moment is not a matter of asking them how they feel. Chances are, they do not yet know. This is a time for keeping them warm, bringing sweet tea, making a space of quiet. The heartbroken may not yet comprehend what has been smashed apart in their world, so the first step is to hold them in this most disorientating coming to consciousness. As with all the stages, shock can come back around when least expected, throwing the griever back into the first moment of collapse. It helps us all to know this can happen.

I see myself through the eyes of others. Too often shocked by what they reflect. I can't quite see what they see but I know I look bad. Something is showing and it is something terrible. So repugnant it makes others shy away from me, avoid my gaze, change the subject, change direction, almost break into a run. Anything other than risk getting caught in the horror I emanate.

In the beginning, I thought I could see the others who were carrying monsters. Ah yes, I thought, this is being really grown-up. In some ways, grief is a kind of superpower. A sort of spider-sense buzzing through your head and nerve endings, responding to the grief of others around you, going into overdrive when someone else's (almost) hidden wound brushes close.

It is also, of course, desperately lonely.

Not because there is anything special about your grief. There isn't, and people are all too eager to remind you of this, even in the first moments when you can't see straight and you hope you are going to wake up soon. Not only the cruel 'it is God's will' types, although they are the most enthusiastic. There's also the 'well I know all about it' and the 'my uncle/neighbour/school friend/workmate had something similar happen and you will get over it or you won't get over it or it was your fault or it must run in your family or I must keep talking to stop the terrifying possibility that you tell me how you feel'.

Because where would we be then? If those truly lost in the madness of grief started to say it out loud?

For a while we go to counselling to try to become functional again, able to move through the steps of looking after our children. Mainly I talk about work. Another job where they wish, more than anything, that I would just go away. We use that space to avoid ever talking about what has happened. Instead we talk about getting alternative employment, or the impact of moving away on our older child, or what redress someone might have in this situation.

But never about what has happened.

KALI, OR A STORY ABOUT SHOCK

The goddess Kali, embodiment of the forces of death and time, is tasked with defeating evil. She is the most fear-inducing of combatants, fuelled by divine strength and quickness, beheading demons with her multiple limbs. When demons threaten to overpower the world, Kali is the one who must save us all, and she takes her responsibility seriously. Despite her divinity, she must engage each demon in hand-to-hand combat, slicing their heads from their bodies and adding them to her garland of severed heads. Somehow it is these trophies, with the still fresh seeping of blood, that re-energise her for the long battles ahead. It is worth noting that all the miscreants are 'men', demons embodied as men, vanquished by the energies of death and time embodied as a kind of feminine being.

When I am told this story as a child, Kali is in a frenzy of righteous busyness. Slice-slice-slicing, one head after another. Stringing them up almost without looking. Because the armies of evil are so numerous and her task is so enormous, who has time to check the details? And that is where the mishap occurs. While raging around the world, plucking demon heads as so many links in her bloody necklace, Kali makes a mistake. A terrible, irreversible mistake that stops the narrative of cleansing vengeance in its tracks. As she strings together her trophy heads, Kali glances down for a moment and sees—and this is a pretty dramatic pause—the head of her own husband hanging in her hands.

She puts her tongue between her teeth, an expression of dismay.

Biting her tongue is the most Bengali of gestures for 'what have I done?'

Although also the most mundane of scolds. 'Ish,' say the grown-ups, 'what have you done now?' and they stick out the tips of their tongues as a gesture showing the outrage of whatever failure or misstep has been spotted.

But for Kali, the tongue between teeth is a freezing forever.

I very much feared that this book would be devoid of laughs, that it might even end up quite pompous. Or twee. Too saccharine to stomach, something that might get in the way of my other out-in-the-world fictions of self. In another incarnation my role is that of gets-laughs-out-of-a-stone thinker/writer. 'Thinker/writer on the left.' I think we all know how miserable such a role can be. And I have been quietly conceited about my reputation for being 'less pompous, sometimes fun'.

I worried that this book might end up spoiling my fun in more than one place. Make it seem like I was really using the gags to cover some deep misery. Maybe even stop people from hearing the jokes at all. There is nothing that could make that worth it for me.

But heartbrokenness lives alongside the relentless vaudeville show of my life. And of many others, I would wager. Not because clowning is an archetypally sad or scary endeavour, although that may also be true. My suggestion is rather that heartbrokenness is only a breath away from the ridiculous. Perhaps they are even one and the same.

We can act as if being ridiculous is permitted only when it is consciously staged. We have space for the clown who perfects their art, or for the wit who bon-mots us into amusement. But ridiculousness without self-awareness—that is a dangerous thing. Appear in the world too many times with your arse showing and, well, things might all collapse.

I have been ridiculous, knowingly and unknowingly. Perhaps always. Certainly for as long as I can remember. I have gone from being caught out and self-conscious (although always too late) to being wilfully silly, someone who can be relied on not to take things too seriously. If making myself ridiculous helps that, well, that too is a contribution. Because being ridiculous—out of control and out of any capacity for control—that too is a shared humanness.

Grief is a loss of dignity. Perhaps it is the state in which we are at our most ridiculous. Bursting with irrationality, desperate for miracles. A grieving human might be the most clownish thing on earth.

But I wonder if the loss of dignity is also something to reclaim. Human dignity is a tricky matter. For some it is the right to be treated as human, to be accorded the simple everyday respect of being seen and allowed to live, to be spared humiliation and the extreme actions that can arise from degradation and life-or-death need.

For others, however, it can be a bit of pose, can't it? Dignity worn too tetchily can be an over-claim, an uncomfortable centring of the self. A code the thin-skinned use to excuse poor behaviour.

Grief will undo all of that. Any delusion you might have about your own strength of character, grief will wash away. Any idea you have about your behaviour in the world, forget it. Grief will make you forget yourself, forget what is and what is not acceptable, forget whether you ate or washed or put your clothes on. It will make you unsure of whether you are awake or sleeping. Whether you have been here before. Make the light seem too bright and smells seem too strange. Grief will make you, in the most disconcerting of ways, forget yourself.

Ecstasy also contains this uncertainty, the same sense of falling, the same dissolution of boundaries. Heartbrokenness edges into the realm of ecstasy, with the same resistance to the loss of self. But before nirvana—and perhaps we do not say this enough—there is the ridiculous.

The careful staging of status, looks, intellect, all the things you might have practised being in the outside world, grief will take away. Maybe not in a crescendo where everyone can see the tragedy and perhaps sympathise with your plight. Oh no, nothing so reasonable.

Instead, grief will steal little bits of what you think of as yourself and put them back together in a different order, jumbling up the habits and attributes and laying them out again so you resemble almost a person. No-one can guess when the breaks will show. When something will drop off, leaving a gaping hole that reveals the whole performance as a circus. Watch any room when the grief-stricken enter. The not-quite-human approximation of normality brings a stink to the air, and everyone rushes to look away for fear of being the first to be frozen in the gaze of this pitiful yet dangerous monster.

Because the heartbroken are scary and the heartbroken are grotesque and the heartbroken are ridiculous.

I want to say being ridiculous can be a state of grace.

Ridiculousness can rely on a forgetting of propriety, and forgetting is a kind of ease. Who cares, after all, about what we look like? What people think of us? Whether our in/difference to the world and others in it shows? Who cares that we no longer care?

There is a journey from presenting a respectable self to the world to ceasing to care what the world thinks of you because the sorrow of heartbreak has made all worldly performances feel heavy and pointless, and who is all this effort for, anyway. And in that gap between stiffening lips and stiffening resolve and a second infancy of leaky bodily disorder, there is the ridiculous.

Sometimes you might witness something in your life that reveals for a brief moment how the ridiculous edges into the beatific. You could look backwards at centuries of beautiful idiots, whatever unspeakable distresses or unnamed disabilities they held, and note that veneration and ridicule can slide into each other, perhaps happen in the same instant. Every time children throw stones and the object of ridicule responds with a smile. Whenever the apparently abject burst into song or laughter or loud scolding of some interlocutor who cannot be seen.

In another time, we might have called this the divine.

DENIAL

Our whole world is structured to deny the existence of unnecessary pain. Sometimes the denial is of the fact that this pain is unnecessary, because we must be persuaded of the unavoidability of making some desperate and expendable. Sometimes the denial is of there being any pain at all, because we want to believe that things are not so bad, perhaps that this is just what life is for everyone. Mainly, the denial is of any alternative. The only way we are permitted to imagine survival is through a normalisation of pain. How silly to suggest anything else could be possible. The encouragement and reward of denial is a tool of class domination. All of the ways of not seeing and not saying, of keeping calm and carrying on. Every time we are applauded for coping so well and trying so hard. Every time we ourselves take secret solace in our own stoicism, because isn't looking on the bright side the very stuff of everyday heroism? Always someone worse off than you, don't you know?

Why do we deny heartbrokenness? Not only in ourselves but in others too.

Perhaps because acknowledging sadness threatens to open us to the abyss, and after that, there is only falling.

But pretending sadness has no role in our political imaginaries takes its own toll. Silencing heartbreak only returns us to the crassest celebrations of strength. Or the most dubious displays of empathy. Sadness appears only as something to fight off or to transform into charity. Almost nowhere do we say to each other, we must travel with our sadness because every dream of a new world requires us to understand we have been broken by the old.

Most of recorded human culture has celebrated pain for some. Sometimes as a document of victory and martial domination. Sometimes as a marker of the apparent coincidence of power and moral worth. Sometimes in order to further mythologies of suffering as cleansing, as godliness, as secular sainthood. We deify endurance across cultures and historical moments.

We know there are horrors in the world. Perhaps our families have lived through some of them. Looking backwards, we see generations of carnage and hardship. And when we acknowledge these histories, we can run close to celebrating pain.

Is trauma the right word for this muting of our own pains?

Learning our histories and honouring our ancestors can mean wading through blood. We learn how much has been lost and feel the weight of survival. It has all been for us, apparently. And so we bite back our own griefs.

Survivor worship is a strange thing. It can make us regard suffering as the marker of a meaningful life. But it can also disallow the everyday grief of more ordinary lives, all the pains that are not part of world-historical events, the mundane losses that happen in any and every life. They become downgraded against the enormity of generations of collective horror. Who are we to nurse our tiny griefs against this backdrop?

Collating the rituals of collective grief, I realise I am looking for a way of making grieving comfortable. Despite myself, I still long for a route to domesticate grief, and reintegrating it into the realm of the community ritual seems like a way of calming the monsters.

But I think I am wrong. We are always stretched between the possibilities and sustenance of collective existence and the abyss of the self. Even the attempt to erase and collapse the self through religiosity is a kind of admission of the knotty irreducibility of the self. Human beings, with all of their emotional softness and irrational attachments and needs, are not so easily collapsed into an undifferentiated mass. We may be interdependent and unable to function without each other. We may be deeply social creatures who spend our whole lives reaching out to touch one another. But we are not machinic components of the collective subject. And whatever commitment we may or may not have to some or other collective project, the lairy and disorientating ride of selfhood cannot be wholly escaped.

Grief can uncover all of that, the extent to which we are not and can never be in command of our own selves.

And that, of course, is why the rituals of collective grief can reference elation or intoxication or disorientation. Not only the blurring of the world of the whirling dervish, but also the whisky bottle on the table, or the light-headedness of the fast.

Grief reminds us, with some violence, that our selves are unbounded, and also that this reminder of unboundedness leads to the very edge of the abyss.

When Freud tells us of the death drive, he is pointing to something in the way that humans both desire and fear oblivion. Freud is trying to make sense of a historical moment of mass carnage but, as was his life's work, tries again to map the threads sewing together collective experience and the lonely self, however loosely and unevenly.

The turning outwards of our fear of grief and its disorientations can result, so obviously, in the violence that scars our world. The will to assert and to invade, to conquer and to quell. It is not hard to see how these recurrent motors in human history reveal a need to demonstrate power and to pretend to be impervious to the pains of loss.

The propriety of grief is highly racialised. Who did not know this? The master races of the earth are allowed their griefs, in carefully scripted terms; perhaps they will be congratulated on their strength and forbearance. The rest of us, well, it is all wailing and mucous-dripping ugly crying and screams behind the death procession.

Fear of the abyss, then, might span the deepest recesses of the psychodrama of selfhood and much more mundane and awkward anxieties about human status. Somewhere between fear of oblivion and fear of what the neighbours might say. Collapsing the distance between the biggest and the smallest questions, as if there were no difference between asking, 'Why am I here?' and asking, 'What do they think of me?'

PUPPET LOVE, OR A STORY ABOUT DENIAL

I accompany my small child to watch *Astro Boy* in the cinema, hoping for the usual semi-conscious cartoon-viewing in the dark. What comes next is not what I expect.

Astro Boy, or his prototype, is the talented, lovable and hyper-intelligent child of a government scientist. One day he visits his father's laboratory, coinciding with some or other empty-headed dignitary interested in the destructive powers of the latest technology. Somehow, in the course of his visit, the boy finds himself enclosed in a testing arena with one of his father's dangerous robots while a demonstration is underway. The robot is set to blast everything in its path, and with the experiment in full swing, we watch the boy die. It is a truly terrible scene, with parent and child trapped on either side of a transparent barrier, unable to reach each other as the robot prepares to eliminate. In response, the father uses his scientific genius to construct a robot replica of his son, and the rest of the film is about the adventures of this not-real boy.

It is a sort of Pinocchio story, except unlike Geppetto, who longs to parent a real child, Astro Boy's father constructs his facsimile child as a replacement for his lost flesh-and-blood offspring. Perhaps longing for the child yet to be born is on a continuum with grief for the child who has been lost.

In *Coppélia*, that other celebrated tale of puppetry as a means of managing heartbreak, the evil alchemist who seeks to steal the hero's soul to bring his mechanical daughter alive is also motivated by a longing for the life of his child. Coppélia is the love object of the inventor, not only of Franz, the slightly questionable young lover who can be distracted from his fiancée by the sight of a beautiful woman blowing him kisses. The story of the lifelike, enlivened automaton circulates as another reminder of our wish to do away with the possibility of loss through manufacture. There is nothing ever that can be lost that cannot be remade, made better. And no subjugation that we will not tolerate for others if it can promise us relief from our own heartbreak.

Puppet love is poignantly tragic, revealing to all the desperate refusal of reason that comes with grief. But it is also a warning of what can be countenanced by the grieving. A willingness to steal another's soul if that can prevent the ordeal of heartbreak.

There is such a pressure to write in predictably heart-pulling ways, perhaps with the excuse to yourself that it is to help others with their own pain. This whole way of speaking to each other about grief has become a growing section of published culture, as if there is something surprising about the experience of loss in a human life. You would have thought that as a species we would have run out of things to say about our grief, because our grief is as ordinary as our breathing or our pissing or our shitting and all of those other almost unconscious actions that make us so unavoidably human.

So, in a bad-temperedly contrary state of mind, I am trying to think about how a person might write about grief in the most objectionable of ways. What could be said to absolutely alienate the reader? How could you talk in a way that offered no solace, that broke the connections between us, that said, everything you feel is nothing like what I feel and when I speak about my grief I want you to doubt your own because even the sharing of grief feels like a belittling of my pain and my loss.

Saying that would only confirm something that in fact we know all too well already: that grief is greedy. Grief makes us the ugliest versions of ourselves. Not only the much-depicted ugly crying, all snot and redness and gnarled-up faces, but also some much deeper ugliness where we admit that lodged within our care for one other there is a marked disinterest in all the other others. Don't talk to me about your loss. I don't care what you have borne. All I care about is my own grief, my own loss, my own special, irreplaceable lost person. Grief can reduce the whole world into no more than mourner and mourned.

I also wanted to write about the strange elation of grief, the near high, feeling like you are flying above the horrors of the world by just surviving this most terrible of things. It can make you reckless. Make you believe that nothing more could ever happen to you. Make you believe you're invulnerable because now you don't even really care what happens next.

All of this is there in accounts of the abyss or the death drive or the moment of ecstatic revelation. When what we most fear hurtles down the highways of our lives, crushing and rendering irrelevant all that we have assembled, threatening to take us from ourselves.

And in that moment, we can no longer distinguish what we fear from what we long for.

Trying to manage the unhappy consciousness of always impending grief pushes us to seek oblivion, a term that could mean nirvana or merciful unconsciousness or death.

But I think what we mean is bliss.

In common with most of the world, my family holds many generations of barely speakable grief.

My paternal grandmother gave birth to thirteen children and saw only six survive to adulthood. My mother's family was displaced by the infamous Bengal famine of 1943, eventually riding the scary overcrowded last-minute trains of Partition time to make sure everyone ended up on the same side of the artificially and hastily created border. My father's family walked out of Burma under British 'supervision', a walk on which many thousands of Indians died. As a child, my mother found herself 'Indian' in an apparently newly independent 'India' but speaking a different language and marked as a refugee, allowed to take water from the well only at the end of the day when all locals had finished. My father's father died of a heart attack before he was forty, while trying to re-establish his family after losing everything when he became a refugee from Burma. My grandmother, married as a child and having lost seven children already, was left with the remaining six. The older daughters went out to work to sustain the family, with all the talk and aspersions that brought upon previously 'respectable' families in the 1940s and 1950s. My mother's baby brother died for lack of a doctor when their mother tried to join her husband in the new place to which he had escaped under cover of night to work and feed his family. This grandmother told me, still smarting from the humiliation decades later, of what it was like to wake up with three tiny children and no husband in a household stretched tight by famine and want. Later her oldest child was diagnosed with schizophrenia and taken from the family home at seventeen to an institution so far away that visits were impossible. When her next child, my mother, married secretly and moved to England, my grandmother let her arthritis take over her body, retreating to her bed and abandoning self-care.

By the time I met her, when she would not yet have been sixty, her back was permanently bent out of shape and her teeth were missing. I was afraid of her and the wayward embodiment of grief that she presented.

Mine is an ordinary family. Our griefs are not spectacular and could be repeated by many across the world.

But once you start to list them out, the weight of a human life seems too much to bear.

My older family members bore the horrors of their lives with varying expressions of anger and detachment. Overall, I think the impact of the collective traumas of famine and displacement has been to mute empathy. Whatever else happened next, some part of them all has been frozen in these life-threatening and uncontrollable moments, with the result that they are always fighting for their lives. Kick first and ask questions later.

In reality, this was never a problem until other, newer, bad things happened.

In mythologies of survival across communities and geography and time, survival can seem like a feat of derring-do. In the face of mass death, every survivor becomes heroic. We imagine ourselves trying to face down death, staying upright somehow while all those around are razed to the ground, and it seems superhuman.

It also seems finite.

Face down the devil once and you are done.

If only it were so easy.

If any even slightly plump brown person appears on television, my other half nudges me and says, 'One of your compatriots.' Annoying, but sadly quite often true.

Bengalis are not the only well-known fatsos of the Subcontinent, but we do have an assured seat at the snack table. On meeting one of us, the non-Bengali South Asian is likely to exclaim, 'Bengali! Rasgulla! Swandesh!' in recognition of our legendary and distinctive sweetmeat culture.

Also known for chattiness, snackery, poetry, rebellion and a lack of business sense, Bengalis are known as a moon-faced race of child-people. Who can be a bit on the pudgy side.

Bengal suffered famine in 1770, 1866, 1873–74 and 1896–97. A famine commission was formed in 1880, the recommendations of which were the basis of the Bengal Famine Code, first published in 1895, which outlined a process for anticipating the onset of famine and a number of tests that should lead to the appointment of a famine commissioner. The Code was a tacit acknowledgement of the role of British rule in creating famine conditions, although it was not anything like an effective tool of intervention. India had suffered a series of major famines throughout the eighteenth and nineteenth centuries, both under the administration of the East India Company and under direct rule, across a number of regions. The creation of famine was so strongly associated with the British rule of India that even the post-independence world of the twentieth century imagined the Subcontinent primarily through the lens of hunger. Bangladesh, in particular, became synonymous with flooding and famine, disasters enragingly rewritten as acts of nature.

The long history of repeated famine leaves a population of those who have survived generations of calorific deprivation. The question of how famine affects future generations requires further scientific investigation, but research into its impact on the individual gives us some indication that undernourishment in both prenatal and early life can increase the likelihood of developing diabetes in later life. I read a baleful popularised account of these findings in an Indian newspaper suggesting that 'South Asians' need to do two and a half times as much exercise as 'Europeans' to reap the same rewards. (I know, don't ask. How can we indulge in these intriguing speculations about how catastrophe remakes the body and not expect the sneaky interloper of race science to be creeping around the edges?) All over the world, soft-bellied brown people read this and look at images of taut blondes running/swimming/biking/trekking and try to imagine themselves doing the same thing but more than twice as far.

As we pass around the consolation snacks, I wonder if we will carry the bodily imprint of historical loss forever.

ANGER

There might be a sudden resurgence of energy now, but not for anything good. Instead, the grieving one might rage around the place, repeating monologic accusations or denunciations or curses. Things might be broken. Friends summoned to be told never to return. Cupboards emptied. Charity bags filled. Bonfires lit to take away every trace of hurtful memory. Sometimes the anger is odder than this. A person might go out to the shops and come back with a story of dragons defeated and wrongs righted, perhaps with some unexplained injuries, or missing an item or a button. Maybe there is a return to work, and the clunking bureaucracy of the workplace (which never worked before either, but that was before this state of rage) is taken on in a new crusade, absorbing the oddly hungry energies of grief and spitting it back out as a (long) series of terse memos. This is a time when nothing sits right and every wrong must be addressed. The inconsequential disagreement with the neighbour about the hedge? In this stage, that means war. Awkward misspeaking about loss at a social event? Time to educate those assembled, because let it pass, and what then? If you ever hear an over-loud voice cowing others with a self-righteous assertion of morality or procedure, there is a good chance it is grief talking.

There is a rage that comes from understanding the depth and breadth of the world's grief. All the waste and the pain and the stumbling on regardless. When you add it up in your head, the unfairness can feel too much to bear. Spinning out across continents and centuries—once we begin to comprehend the enormity of loss, including the most unnecessary and cruel, what is there to feel but rage?

I am angry to be so broken. This is not what the stories tell us. For us, we survivors, we warriors, grief is no more than another battle. Only triumph is to be recorded. Yes, there are demons, but are we not from a long line of demon-slayers? The lesson is, always, that grief is something to overcome.

So what am I to do with these other strange hauntings? Some are easy. Hair falling out—so what, let it fall. Unexpected rashes and bruises—wear long sleeves. Unable to close your eyes to sleep—paint on an alternative face and nod your way through a blurry waking day.

But what about the other things?

For a while I keep falling over. A literal stumbling at the hurdles of living. I think I know where this one starts but, awkwardly, not where it ends. On the day I come out of hospital, I try to walk down our road, and the pavement slips away from me. I have been lying down for eleven days and outside only briefly in an ambulance. It isn't grief, it is just a loss of coordination. But still that sense of falling stays with me. Not as a failure, actually. For a while I believe I am flying, not falling. That this is another superpower shared by the grief-stricken.

In common with other bookish types, I have always existed partly in the shadows. Skulked around the edges of things. Chosen quiet times and deserted places. Enjoyed the gloomy nooks and crannies of life. Maybe assumed that this was true for everyone and learned to have just enough of a daytime public face to pass, while I retreated to my own elsewheres. *And this was something I always enjoyed: the ability to maintain a secret elsewhere life.* Grief sends us back to our ill-lit other lives. To dreams. To curtains drawn and company avoided. To the realm where fantasy, memory and haunting meld. And sometimes this return might feel like a relief.

In reality, I was not angry. I never for a moment said, why me? Why us? Why him? Why not someone else? What have we done to anger the gods? How can life be so unfair? I knew better than all of that. Instead I thought, now it has come, the horror that is always on the horizon, and what right have I or anyone else to pretend that we are above such vulnerability?

So, nothing to be angry about. Maybe a passing anger at myself and the thin dreams of invulnerability. An anger at our hopefulness for human life as we reach out and make things anew. How very stupid, how very, very stupid of us to think that our efforts can ever scrape us away from the dust that we are.

But I know there was an anger around me that made me afraid. Eruptions of aggression from almost strangers and awkward colleagues. They were angry with me, I understand now. Angry at the reminder I was of the bad things that can happen. Grief can be angry in unexpected ways, and I wonder if fear of the grieving is a fear of justified and absolutely legitimate anger. As if standing near those deep in grief might pull you into their conflagration, burn you up in their horror before you even have the chance to live through your own. I know people also felt that they might catch mortality from standing near us, and I wonder if that happens to everyone who grieves in an unexpected order, at a time that makes them show their grief too openly to be accommodated into polite rituals.

But you can't catch heartbrokenness from another, whatever you might fear. What that lashing out and running away and behaving cruelly is telling you about yourself is that the heartbreak is already there—still dormant, perhaps, but certainly there. It is our destiny. And no amount of viciousness towards those in grief will keep you safe from it.

When I talk about heartbrokenness as the class consciousness of racial capitalism, I am in part poking fun at a long history of theorising. Theorisations of class consciousness as a serious and scientific matter place it at the heart of how we might imagine revolutionary change, asserting that it is only through class consciousness, when the class agent fully realises itself to become the infamous class for itself, that such change can be achieved. And in this account, we must understand that class consciousness is far more than just a feeling. Perhaps there is something implied about shared lives, shared emotions and shared circumstances in the idea of a class in itself and for itself, but this isn't a story about heartbreak.

I want to suggest that heartbrokenness is a better and more apt description of class consciousness under racial capitalism because the accounts of racial capitalism help us to understand how we are divided from each other. The theorisation of racial capitalism is precisely a theorisation of how capital segments, divides and differentiates populations. It is a story about the confounding of solidarities and the atomisation of everyday life, and within that, the reaching for the scientific insight of class agency or the realisation and coming to consciousness of the class agent seem to fall away. There is no one story or one location through which the violences of racial capitalism bring us all together. Not bringing us together—disallowing the coming together—is what characterises the disciplinary techniques of racial capitalism across space and time. Heartbreak runs through it all.

Again, as I have said before too often, the story of racial capitalism teaches us that we are all living shitty lives but in different ways. Heartbrokenness opens the possibility of registering these scattered pains, perhaps to begin to comprehend their odd and changing interconnections. Something in the near ecstasy of the loss of self can begin an opening to others. Something in the confusions of misery/bliss can become conscious of a collectivity that cannot yet be narrated. Something in being heartbroken that lets us finally begin to see each other.

WISHES, OR A STORY ABOUT ANGER

Everyone knows this story—one of my favourites for so long and always good for a laugh.

A poor couple go through some or other unexpected action: rubbing a lamp, repeating an incantation, throwing salt or pepper or herbs over this or that shoulder, jumping over the broomstick, catching the eye of a black cat. You know the kind of thing, almost mundane, something you might do by accident. And then—quite suddenly—magic appears. Ta-da!

For this pair, their action—which releases some imprisoned magical being from captivity, I think—leads to the granting of three wishes. Life-changing stuff for anyone. More so for the hungry and bedraggled, wracked with cold and want and exhaustion from the effort of keeping alive.

The bloke, poor soul, cannot contain himself.

'I wish for a big fat juicy sausage!'

They have been sitting over their almost meal, thin gruel, bare scraps, plates all but empty.

The woman, another poor soul, cannot contain herself either. Her rage flies out of her mouth, and before she knows it—

'You old fool! I wish that sausage were stuck on the end of your nose.'

And there they are. Still cold, still hungry, still poor. One with an enormous sausage growing out of his nose.

If ever there was an image of unbearable irritation, surely this is it. Each knowing that the other has put them in this predicament. Each knowing that their own foolishness has sewn them into this tight place.

They spend some time trying to find a way out. The woman tries hard to persuade the man that it is not so bad, not so very noticeable. Certainly something that could be lived with if the last wish were used to provide for a more comfortable life. She is begging him: *learn to live with your sausage-nose so we can eat every day and be warm and have a home and hot water and a rest. Get over yourself.*

This pause in the story feels endless. What can we accommodate ourselves to? What can compensate for the twin wounds of disfigurement and loss of dignity? What other lives can we imagine if only …?

Of course, he decides he cannot live with his sausage-nose. The last wish is used up to make the sausage disappear.

The story ends as it began. Two hungry, shivering people, looking at their empty plates.

BARGAINING

This is the stage of if onlys. If only I had seen a doctor, eaten my vegetables, told them I loved them, carried out good deeds. What makes it the stage of bargaining is the belief, however weakly held, that there is still a bargain to be struck. If I can just perform the required action or pay the demanded price, perhaps grief can be sent packing. This is the time of trying to make deals with God—that most hapless of human endeavours. But it is also a time of multiple adjustments and new leaves turned. A time when the heartbroken will try just about anything. As you can understand, this makes them both exciting and dangerous to be around. In our world of multiple heartbreak, including within the one lifetime, bargaining can seem like the whole business of life. Forever trying to strike a deal with the forces massed against you. Always looking for an angle, because the small cracks and crevices of the unexpected angle are all there is to nurture us. A person might do some really foolish and outlandish things in this phase. Most of the time, that is also OK.

PERSEPHONE, OR A STORY ABOUT BARGAINING

When I was small, my mother told me often the story of Persephone, a story I found very scary. In the retelling, I understood the story as follows:

1. Scary man, Hades, sees, wants and abducts young girl, Persephone, carrying her off to the underworld, where she cannot be found.
2. Wild with grief, the girl's mother, Demeter, tears around searching for her daughter. Demeter's sorrow casts a shadow over the whole world so that nothing grows any more. The earth and its people grieve with Demeter as everywhere falls into famine and want.
3. Meanwhile, in the darkness of the underworld, Persephone is also grieving for her mother and her mother's pain of loss. How she expresses her grief and her defiance is by refusing to eat. Hades brings her every delicacy, but she will allow nothing to pass her lips, and, in an echo of the fading away of life on earth, Persephone also starts to fade.
4. A bargain must be struck to prevent the loss of all life. Persephone will be allowed to return to her mother. This is the part of the story most loved by my own mother, where the mutual joy of reunion between parent and child brings spring back to earth. Because that is what love is like, rejuvenating in ways that can claw back life

and make things grow again even when it feels as though everything is lost.

5. But there is a catch. Persephone has not managed, understandably, to refuse all food in the underworld. In a moment of weakness, she allowed herself to eat six pomegranate seeds. I hear this as an example of Hades' sneakiness, for the pomegranate was presented as part of the most delectable of fruit platters, designed to entice Persephone with the flavours and aromas of home. In the end, she ate a little not to appease her hunger but as an expression of homesickness.
6. The bargain of her return, a negotiation undertaken with her captor and abuser, is that she may go home only if she has not partaken of any of the fruits of the underworld. Looking back, I guess the story is that eating the foods of the realm of death makes it impossible to make the journey back to life. Because Persephone has consumed these tiny morsels, the compromise is that she must return to Hades each year. I hear this as six months at a time, a month for each seed, but other tellings say it is one or three. For the period when Persephone must return to her rapist-husband, Demeter grieves again, and it is winter on earth.

This bargain with grief is also an accommodation. Live with sorrow for part of the year and the bargain is that spring will come. Perhaps it is learning to live with sorrow that brings spring into being. It is only in the face of horror that we see the extent of what love can do: what it can stop, and what it can make.

How do we mourn lost love?

When you saw the word 'heartbroken', this is what you thought the book would be about, isn't it? Don't be sheepish. We all know romantic disappointment is the mode of heartbreak that most swirls around our public consciousness, taking up almost all the space and seeping into all and any language we have to say what it is to be painfully sad. This is the human sadness that suffuses the laments of popular song, standing in for every form of human longing.

The world has devised many remedies for this kind of broken-heartedness.

The most optimistic suggest that there has not been or need not be any loss at all.

A love potion with a lock of the beloved's hair or perhaps some unlikely and cruel concoction of animal parts. An incantation by the light of the moon. A lucky charm under your pillow or next to your skin. An irrational ritual in the cause of hope.

One side of mourning lost loves takes this form of trying to get them back. Stop this hurt by bringing my love home to me. Show them the error of their ways. Or cast a spell so they cannot remember what they did or why they did it.

I try to find the details of half-remembered ancient recipes for sure-fire lovespells and find, to my surprise, countless providers of new magic. Often these guides rework old potions and rituals, referencing the earlier origins of their slightly outlandish advice. Sometimes, with an admirable audacity, they claimed to be harnessing the new possibilities of contemporary technologies by extending the powers of ancient magic through the internet. Some themes I remember from a much earlier time, including:

1. The usefulness of having a lock of your beloved's hair, or some other personal item. You might end up burning this and burying it in a significant and/or auspicious place, such as under a very big tree.
2. That you need to choose whom you are casting your spell on. You cannot just use a scattergun approach and hope the magic will stick somewhere. Most advisers are very insistent on this point.
3. The fashioning of likenesses of your loved one and yourself to be tied together, perhaps with incantations, perhaps with the burning of something aromatic, perhaps with the eating of something sweet.

The discerning reader will have understood already that these methods seek to overturn the pain of loss by making the loved one return. However unlikely, the convoluted details of ingredients and rituals do present a welcome focus of busyness for the lovelorn. Something like funeral arrangements for lost romance, with the hope that once the mourner has walked through the steps of the ritual, the passing of time and effort of activity will bring them to a different place in their grief.

When still in the throes of early-ish grief, I heard a radio programme where women mourned the ends of their marriages as a result of infidelity.

I thought, unkindly, that their grief was just a kind of petulance. Not much more than a blow to their pride; upset at the loss of their marriages as a kind of property.

I did think at the time that if I were one of their husbands, I too would run away as fast as I could, with whatever or whoever might take me. With hindsight, I know this to be a moment of cruelty in my own grief. I know, of course, that people become broken if the life they hoped to live is taken away, sometimes smashed to pieces in front of them. But, also, the urge to flee is so understandable. Who can bear the weight of being another's sandbag against grief?

I wonder if our culture of endlessly reported and celebrated romantic disappointment is a wilful displacement of our knowledge of other, more permanent forms of loss.

Romance serves as a proxy through which we can practise the experience of grief. Think about how we talk about loss. The songs, the poetry, the films. The everyday philosophies of heartbroken living. *Sit with your grief, remember the good times, cut yourself some slack.* Lost love is the refrain that whooshes through our culture as our shorthand for what the sadnesses of life might feel like. It is the form of grief that we speak, repeatedly. The very business of being alive, because we must all love and lose and that is what being alive means.

All of this—I put it to you in my most extravagantly lawyerly voice—shows that romantic love and its loss serve to redirect our terror of grief. A displacement, a practice run and, of course, *of course*, a distraction.

Because romantic disappointment trains us to walk through the stages and performances of grief. Like the death of childhood pets, perhaps. Or the cathartic release of the shameless weepie, the one where the reviewer chirps, 'Don't forget your hanky!' Looking at the whole glittery edifice of romantic love, commodified beyond any other aspect of life, rammed into every waking moment, wedged into the business of our dreams, I wonder if the whole point of all of that is to provide a proxy for grief.

I know this sounds cruel. As if lost love is no loss at all. My imaginary friend. My hamster. My marriage. All proxy losses training us for death.

Of course, I am only joking. In part, at least. Heartbreak is a grief that can break people. Unlike death or illness or disaster, lost love feels like pain caused on a whim. The love object could as easily love us as not, could as easily be with us as with anyone else. So the grief cannot be soothed by a sense of the inevitable. Because there is nothing inevitable about lost love.

That is the whole punchline of the romance industry, isn't it? That we can and will find the love of our life, and that in this magical moment, all danger of heartbreak and abandonment will be dispelled?

The difficulty comes with the overvaluation of romantic love in our world. Not for everyone, not all the time, but broadly, this is the consolation that capitalism proffers for our broken lives.

I want to call it romantic disappointment. Play it down. Just another of life's little defeats. As if they have just run out of your favourite flavour, or you find yourself having to wait for the next bus.

But that is clearly not how it feels. People's hearts stop.

Broken-heart syndrome, or takotsubo cardiomyopathy, replicates the symptoms of a heart attack but leaves no trace. It is a practice run—going through the experience of oblivion but surviving.

In less unkind moments, I understand lost love brings its own heartbreak and that this, too, can thin skins enough to become open to others. Although the commodification of romantic love seeks to confine us within the most solipsistic ways of being, the insistent sharing about romantic heartbreak might also lead to a breaking open of the romantic dyad. And just as romantic loss provides a synecdochic reference to all loss, the expression of mourning for lost love enables a collective language of sorrow in the face of love.

But, at the same time, romantic loss contains heartbrokenness and splits it away from the world shaped by violence and want. We learn that this loss is to be met with a wry smile, in the process erasing the losses that should be met with rage.

Sometimes we might try to persuade ourselves that our grief is 'useful'. Useful to the movement; useful as a way of walking in another's shoes, even when we know full well that the sharp lump in our shoes is our own pain and not anyone else's.

Making our grief meaningful is a particularly cruel stage of delusion. Most of all when we pretend that we are doing all this, all of this pretence of surviving, in honour of the ones lost. Because in our hearts we know this show of courage is just another way for us to keep our lost love alive.

Perhaps grief is always a reminder of the frailty of our own bodies. Every loss is also a nudge to see our own corpse in the future. Even our own grief-stricken reflections anticipate those who will mourn us in a time to come. Sometimes the rituals of death incorporate these questionable anticipatory elements, so as we think about legacy, we also think about reputation. Perhaps a tiny part of us quantifies popularity and love and numbers and attendance for those left behind. At its very worst, then, grief makes our whole lives seem trivial. So trivial that the marking of a life seems an affront to common sense.

But for those stuck, for now, in the land of the living, let me tell you: the rituals of grief might be the only thing that can split the endless expanse of time ahead into something manageable. Being seen to grieve and to attend and to mourn and to memorialise is part of reaching acceptance.

When I say acceptance, I mean nothing more ambitious than the longed-for state of just about getting by. Not efficiency. Not achievement. Certainly not providing role models or inspiration. *Just about getting by.* Being able to eat, a little, whatever it might be, at least some of the time. Sleeping occasionally, however much our sleep rages with demons and monsters. Seeing another human being without it bringing the urge to recoil. Speaking and recognising that odd, whiny sound as our own voice and still keeping going. Noticing the world. Not falling over.

A little more than going through the motions, but certainly the point where you feel, with some confidence, that the motions will go on being completed even when moments of horror bubble up.

DEPRESSION

If any of the stages seems to seep into what we expect, or don't expect, from everyday life under late(r) capitalism, then depression is the one. So we know the signs only too well. Persistent low mood. Loss of enthusiasm and energy. Absence of enjoyment. Disrupted eating and sleep. Listlessness. Sometimes it seems as if it is only in the phase of depression that a person can get the performances demanded of the 'worker-citizen' about right. As you stare into space and stop going for lunch, expect your boss to remark on 'how well you are coping'. One of the tricky aspects of this stage is that the heartbroken may well be at their lowest but their behaviour appears more amenable to those around them. Depressed heartbreak is rarely disruptive or demanding or loudly eccentric. Depressed heartbreak is taking a step into death while looking like you have remembered how to behave. I think this tells us something about the half-deadness this world demands of us. Learning to go through the motions and not hope too much.

SALAD, OR A STORY ABOUT DEPRESSION

The story of Rapunzel begins because the mother cannot or will not eat. Nothing has passed her lips for too long, and her husband must watch her fade away before him, unable to rouse her to re-engage with life. It is this wilful falling into death that triggers the fateful trespass that makes the story commence.

What I remember is that the mother longs for the most delicious of salads. Hard for a child to understand, no? That the foodstuff you long for, the boundary between preferring to be dead and clinging on to life, could be green leaves?

In later life, the magical properties of the salad make more sense. In a reversal of the bargain that tricks Persephone into piecing out her freedom in morsels of fruit, the longing for a particular and elusive salad leaf is a marker of still being aligned with the world of the living. The mother hovers near to her death, almost gone, seemingly unwilling to help herself. She has entered a state where her love of life is losing to the allure of death. Only a memory of the taste of green leaves that sprout from the ground, a kind of metaphor for the life force of the earthly world, keeps her from falling back completely into the arms of oblivion.

In the face of this, the woman's husband undertakes the most risky of trespasses. Entering the enclosed garden of the witch or the monster, stealing a handful of those delicious leaves. Of course, the story is that to steal back his beloved to the realm of life, the couple must relinquish their first-born. And so, Rapunzel becomes the name of one form of imprisoned femininity, the beautiful girl hidden away from the rest of the world.

As a child, I think I understood this as a story of betrayal. The father betrays the child by choosing the mother, often told as a matter of indulging his wife's whims. Perhaps the mother betrays the child by slipping back into life, back from the very brink, while sacrificing the child's future. But I wonder if it is really a story about moving beyond the stasis of depression, in the process accepting the terrible reality that your children will also live lives of sorrow.

Grief can feel like flying. Or falling. Or flying and falling, with your body shooting out into a flurry of uncountable shreds, ripping apart until there is no trace of what went before. It can feel like disappearing, and the disappearance is a relief, perhaps the first relief for so long, and then you are guilty at the ebbing of pain and pinch yourself back into existence.

So, it starts again. Falling, flying, flailing. Lose yourself and feel less, so feel less bad. Shake yourself back into respectable pain.

Fall again.

And again.

And again.

Survive in this stage for long enough and you can begin to feel like a superhero.

Perhaps we are learning to sit more easily with what Mary Oliver calls the soft animals of our bodies.[3] I notice a greater tolerance of animalistic yearning. An acknowledgement in many places that this is also what we are, gravitating towards bodily comfort or release even as we try our best to keep the rituals of social propriety in play.

I have always been clumsy and uncomfortable in my body. Not only the overt attributes of gender but also just the meaty unwieldiness of an object that seems so far from my thoughts yet in which I have to live.

Grief split me still further from my coordination. I think this is quite common. Strange stigmata in the morning. Scrapes along my limbs. Scratches in places that no-one could reach. For a long time I found it hard to retain spatial awareness. How to walk down any space without bumping into the sides and the objects? How to place your feet without tripping over immediately? How to live in a world where it seemed at any moment the floor could come rushing up to your head? What your body needs and wants becomes so much more mysterious. Eating nothing or eating only one thing. Sometimes cramming your mouth full of sweets or chocolate or cheese or some other childish indulgence. Being given meals of kindness and chewing a few mouthfuls tastelessly. Washing more sporadically. Forgetting how to wash. I was definitely showering, but somehow the efficiency of my washing rolled right back to early childhood. Which bits do you do? How do you do the bits that are hard to reach? How do you know when you're done? How can you tell when you're dirty? And I know I looked dishevelled. Perhaps a trace of that dishevelled moment is still with me today. Maybe that too is part of the humanness of knowing grief in another. All of the hairs out of place, a slight dirtiness

3 Mary Oliver, *Wild Geese: Selected Poems*, Tarset: Bloodaxe, 2004.

around the edges. Dishevelment can be part of how you show other people that you know there are more important things in life than this.

Perhaps the pandemic has reminded us all of our animal selves, returning us to soft flesh. Perhaps living through a pandemic has brought the experience of growing old into the lives of the young, pushing an awareness of mortality into places which should, in all fairness, be awash with hormone-charged excess. Instead of feeling invincible, now everyone of all ages has been reminded, too insistently, of our shared frailty.

Animality is part of this. Something uncertain about species boundaries. Something about humans in an age of zoonotic disease. Something about the climate emergency. Something about our own bodies and their unpredictable eruptions and slowings-down.

I believed I stank of piss for a long time. I was not trying to be disgusting on purpose, although my ability to remember and complete the rituals of everyday cleanliness was impaired. For a while I thought this was another price of age. Survive long enough and your body will turn on you in these ways, puncturing any vanity you have left, making the smells and sounds and awkward shedding of aging apparent to all who come close.

(Now I think no-one around me was prepared for what giving birth twice in ten and a half months could do to a body in its forties. So, if this is happening to you or to someone you know, please seek help.)

No-one wants to become aware of the decay of their own body. But that too is part of understanding our limits and mortality. Grace in the face of frailty. But not only grace, with all its connotations of stoicism, but also a different courage. Not a flashbang demonstration of overcoming, or even a quiet battling alone. The part of feeling your own body's decay that counts, really counts, is the part where you find the soft animal. Because that is the part that might change what and how we are to each other.

I want to argue that an awareness of death is at the heart of all emancipatory politics and underpins all attempts at living an ethical life.

But even writing such a pompous phrase makes me pause to giggle. 'Living an ethical life.' Frankly, as the old joke goes, what could make life feel more painfully endless? Being good might not make you live longer, but it will surely make the time pass more slowly.

Being bad, though—really hurtfully, sadistically bad, or bad in ways where you are barely aware of the damage you cause, or bad as an expression of your own deep hurts that you have no ways to address—being bad doesn't save you from loss, and neither does it render you immortal. Perhaps revelling in badness might promise the elation of knowing the gods are, if not dead, at the very least looking away. More often, I think, casual or insistent cruelty works to devalue everything that anyone could ever hold dear, because then the pain of loss is lessened.

Extending the realm of the sacred increases the danger of heartbreak. If every element of the world is enchanted, we feel the loss more keenly. If, on the other hand, the world and its inhabitants are spoiled through wilful neglect or violence or outright terror, then the sense of loss can be contained. Perhaps we even begin to believe that leaving this fallen world is a relief. When we dream of making the world better, we open ourselves to enchantment again. And the almost unbearable danger of enchantment is that the magic will end. The fairies will crumble to dust in our hand. The light will fade. The wonder will retreat, and we will be left bereft again.

Every doctrine of violence and machinery of reaction has relied on how frightening it is to contemplate the crushing of hope. Far safer to expel hope altogether. More sensible than the painful un-numbing of imagining other possibilities.

The other side rely on our resignation, and we are resigned to this fallen world because the scale of the loss would be unbearable if we were ever to acknowledge that each life, each moment, every one of us is a thing of enchantment. Because how, then, could we ever see the carnage and the cruelty and the wrecking of all that is beautiful and hold ourselves together at all?

The fear of even greater heartbreak keeps us in our place and keeps us divided from each other. What if you were really me and I was really you, if the boundaries between us dissolved until there was no longer any difference between my interests and yours? What if we are already as one and have only to see it?

And what if the elation and the ecstasy from this loss of self, which is also a finding of self, as each one of us delights in the coming home of being a part in the whole, what if a world made magical again can also be lost? Well, that really would be a loss, wouldn't it? A loss greater than we can imagine. Perhaps greater than we can bear, greater than anyone could bear, the drip-drip-drip of reaction whispers. How childish to think otherwise. What kinds of fools hope when the wise already know that hopes are made to be dashed?

Our fear of heartbreak is used against us so often and in such painfully ingenious ways.

So dreaming a new world requires a reckoning with heartbreak.

We, the heartbroken, must help each other to live with heartbreak and the fear of heartbreak. Otherwise, the risk of abandoning familiar pains for the unknown is too much for anyone.

It sounds like self-help, doesn't it?

However understandable the turn to self-care, let me say here that the mutual recognition and acceptance of heartbrokenness is not this. Much of the time, living with and helping others to live with heartbreak does not even make us feel better. It is certainly far from the varieties of distraction or wilful forgetting marketed as routes to feeling less bad. A reckoning with heartbreak requires something more and different from these desperate survival strategies.

Without making space for heartbreak, how can we remember why we long for change? But equally, when making space for heartbreak, how can we avoid being frozen by sorrow?

I don't think the ways of talking about emotional turbulence that arise as ways to function in the unhappy present can be enough for those of us trying to remake the world. I know we are also unwell. Often, all too often, self-medicating. Often trying to make lives in the debris of extreme trauma. Haunted by violence we have suffered or witnessed.

But I do think something shifts when we acknowledge our individual but interconnected heartbrokenness.

Unexpectedly, grieving people can laugh quite a lot. Sometimes they laugh in ways that embarrass others. Sometimes they laugh in a way that is mixed up with tears. A little bit frightening in a way we might have thought hysterical in another time. But there is certainly laughter. Sometimes wild, sometimes silly, sometimes just out of relief.

When we think of gallows humour, we tend to think of the transmutation of deadly contracts to more everyday drudgery. After all, none of us really faces the gallows on a day-to-day basis. What we do face is annoying, but less deadly. The slow drip-drip-dripping away of our life force. A disrespect for our time, time that is so clearly limited by mortality. An off-handedness that lets us know we are already as good as dead, so replaceable that our betters barely raise their heads to clock us before consigning us to an imagined grave and a younger, quicker, more compliant replacement. In the face of all this, gallows humour is a way of reinserting our knowledge of death into the extreme irritations of the still living.

But I'm not sure any of that is really joking around about grief. Can people also laugh about their grief itself? Are there jokes to be told? Perhaps there are not outright jokes, with all the performance and scripting and expectation of some other as the audience, but there are all kinds of ridiculous and lighter moments as people move through grief. A kind of light-headedness where all the brakes are off. And although we still live in a world where people can be so, so painfully embarrassed by the grief-stricken, the grieving quite often ignore that and take advantage of their temporary status as living saints or crazed lunatics or wild-eyed harpies. Grieving is an excuse to park reason for a while, and when you park reason, all kinds of entertaining silliness can enter the room.

When I was a lot younger, someone told me a joke, partly in Punjabi (a language I do not speak). Broadly, it goes like this:

A family gathers around the deathbed of a beloved elder, let us say grandfather. Aware that there are only moments left, the grandfather asks of his bedside audience, 'Are you all here?'

'Yes, yes, we are all here, of course, of course.'

'Is my brother here? Playmate and rival and companion throughout my life, holder of our family secrets?'

'Yes, of course, brother, I am here.'

'Is my wife here? Mother of our children, holder of dreams, the girl who stole my heart and kept it as her own?'

'Yes, yes, I am here, my love. Please calm yourself and conserve your energy.'

'Is my son here? Apple of my eye, tall and broad and strong, my hope for the future that can still be built?'

'Yes, father, of course, I am here by your side. You know you can count on me.'

'And my grandchildren, are they all here?'

'Yes, yes, yes,' comes the chorus. 'We are all here to show our love for you.'

'My cousins?'

'Of course.'

'Our lifelong neighbour, whose children grew up alongside our own?'

'Yes, yes, I am here.'

'Really? You are all here? Every one of you?'

'Yes, yes, we are all here, here at your side.'

'Then who is looking after the shop?!'

Much later, an older friend laughs when I retell the story, knowing the ending already ... because this is also a famous Jewish joke.

In either telling, it is a puncturing of grief and the pomposity that impending death can bring. Maybe it is a joke on the teller—'ha ha, look what we are like!' But it is also a reminder of the mundane demands of living that continue despite death.

Whatever we are living through and dying from, someone somewhere will need to mind the shop.

Jokes about heartbreak can work like this, puncturing the enormity of grief with a reminder of the ordinary. Maybe the bills pile up and the phone goes unanswered, but everyone needs to buy toilet paper some time.

Everyone knows the sex lives of the grief-stricken can be erratic, compulsive, desperate.

Be careful with them, and try to forgive their awkward passes as they clutch at intimacy.

If you are living through grief with your lover, retreat to bed when you can, when and if you can both bear it. When you haven't been opening the curtains anyway, so why not? Perhaps no-one is exactly feeling 'sexy', but make space for any and all physical comfort. If possible, try to fuck your partner as if they are a stranger, so the raw wounds of intimacy can be avoided and everyone can manage a few minutes of post-coital sleep.

On the whole, I think lust gets a bad rap from 'The Left'. This isn't helped by the widespread and largely ignored sexual exploitation within many leftist organisations. But lust—the longing for sexual contact with another, often a particular other—has its place in the imagining of a new world and probably always has.

Living with heartbrokenness might also include making space for our unruly and irrational longing for sexual contact, so often with the wrong people in the wrong place at the wrong time. Whatever we do to try to minimise harm from these eruptions, I doubt that we can eradicate the longing.

In my long-past youth, some would talk of post-revolutionary sex with a kind of reverence. Then, in this utopian future, we will be perfectly satiated through forms of union that escape the instrumentalism and objectification of sex shaped by commodification. Sexual exploitation will disappear, as will assorted minor cruelties arising from reducing another to your object.

But I wonder about all of this.

Desire is a tricky and unpredictable thing, and its trippy discombobulation is not so easily banished. We, imperfect humans, like it. And whether or not we want it, we do not control its hold over us. There is something in its compulsion that, like grief, opens us up in ways that make our interdependence apparent.

So make space for desire, even when it feels out of control. Because that embarrassing vulnerability, so differently excruciating to romantic longing, is also part of the heartbrokenness that lets us catch a glimpse of each other and what we, one day, might be.

TESTING

This is the point where someone is no longer surprised to find grief squatting in their consciousness. Perhaps they have become used to this way of existing. Perhaps grief manifests itself as a cranky companion, annoying but familiar. Heartbreak still looks conspicuously uneasy, but it is coming to take its place in and alongside the other business of life. This is the careful, bit-by-bit process of putting weight on a slowly healing fracture again. Unlike the stage of bargaining, there is no appeal to God or any other powerful other here. The heartbroken understands that there is no going back. The tests are not spells or forms of magic. There is no imagined transaction—if I do this, then I will get this other longed-for thing in return. Instead, there are steps towards living with heartbreak. This stage comes as a form of advice. Try to find some ways of practising your return to life in your altered state of heartbreak. Practise them. Increase the weight slowly, as in any sensible training programme. Accept there will be bad days and allow yourself some rest. Keep going.

GHOSTS, OR A STORY ABOUT TESTING

Every ghost story in history is a story about testing. The dead test their altered state—*is that corpse really me?*—while the living try, and largely fail, to live with the spectre of death.

Ghosts are how we talk to each other about the blurry edges between living and dying. Sometimes we might manage to excise the fear a little. Conjure up Casper the Friendly Ghost and, instead of collapsing in the encounter with the spirit of a dead child, see something playful in the refusal to abandon the realm inhabited by the living. Sometimes we might remember that the pull of the living world is the pull of love. Make a thousand tear-jerking movies about ghosts who return for just long enough to put things right or to comfort their loved ones to the point where they can move on. Perhaps we tell the ghost story in its most straightforward incarnation as a tale of outright horror, all slamming doors and other-worldly shrieks, in the end realising that the horror is the anguish of a soul that cannot come to rest—an anguish that comes, more often than not, from the horrors of the living world.

When my mother was a tiny girl, still free to roam barefoot in the open fields and forests of her idyllic early childhood, her grandmother would tell her ghost stories. My mother makes the face of being a small person simultaneously entranced and afraid, big saucer-eyes, hanging on to every word. One story was about the adventures of two white ghosts who lived in a nearby tree: Hono and Lulu. I know, I know, you have to imagine a playful old Bengali granny giggling to herself as she tells it, including the names that no tiny child would suspect to be a joke. Hono and Lulu have a lot of larks, getting up to mischief, flying about the place, doing magic. Usual high jinks of the undead.

My mother speaks of them as her first conception of white 'people'. Unlike my father's family, who had seen British soldiers, my mother inhabited a universe where the land under 'British rule' was populated by fantastical creatures who were never seen. Who knows? Perhaps they did fly and live in trees. How disappointing the realities of whiteness must have seemed.

By now, you know that you have been broken and rebuilt by grief. You know others have lived with this forced remaking. Time to see what you can do with your grief-modelled self.

Maybe you have some grief role models by now. Maybe you want to be a grief role model. Now when you tell the story of your grief, you start to place it in a much longer story of collective loss and pain. Maybe you start to believe you can prevent anyone else from ever feeling like this, that this will be your contribution, as grief-healer and magical fixer of pain. Maybe you start to kid yourself that knowing the historical and political context that created your loss can inoculate against future pain. Maybe the process of testing your theory of healing through extending political consciousness wrecks your head so much that you are thrown right back to the start, where you cannot quite believe that this horror has happened to you and will be your life from now on.

Sometimes the words don't come. There's lots of noise in my head, with competing voices speaking over each other until there's only the hum-hum-hum bursting out of my ears. It feels like nothing comes out into the world, but I am transfixed by the cacophony of noises in, alongside and outside of myself. How can I break into so much noise? I can hardly hear myself think. Trying to frame a sentence feels like looking up at a sheer height; however much I imagine myself at the top, the steps of the journey there elude me. There are so many words shooting around in my head, grabbing any one of them as a starting point is more than I can manage. Sometimes people are waiting for me to respond but I can't fall back on my usual tricks of grunting or saying something non-committal or cracking a weak joke. I am stuck in the storm of my own head, and every external prod only makes the noise more excruciating. Sometimes people ask me things that surely can have no answer: how my year has been, how I'm feeling, how it is to be back. Silence seems like a reasonable response. Perhaps the only possible response.

I know some people are selectively mute, and I wonder if in childhood I was this as well. Although I am sure I did speak, so many people said that they never heard me do so. What I think about people who find it hard to speak in public is that their head is probably tying their tongue, with so many voices struggling to get out that nothing can be heard at all. Sometimes now when things get very bad, I try to shut down my outside self and slip in amongst the inside voices, because although that can be disorientating, it is also euphoric. Like carrying all the dramas and wisdom of the universe playing on your inner screen endlessly for no-one's delectation but your own. Why would I want to hear or speak to anyone else? Of course, now that I am an old and occasionally functioning adult who speaks for a living quite often, people remark upon my facility with speech. So fluent, so articulate, always pulling out just the right word before anyone else. It is a strange thing to come late in life to being a speech giver. I don't know if it means I have tamed the inside voices. Learned how to channel the most publicly entertaining ones into the right space at the right time. Perhaps my self-contained and silent self has died and now exists only as the fleshy puppet of the most insistent of my inner voices. Maybe that's what being a grown-up means, that you stopped doing the thing that feels comfortable and that you want to do and instead drag out of your bag of tricks the thing that seems most appropriate for the context.

Quite often, I think one day I am going to return to the near silence and aloneness. Or that when I'm out in the world—parenting, working, moving through the supermarket and to the bus stop, doing the things that grown-ups do—the cacophony of voices will come to an end sooner than I think. And what then?

For much of human existence (that we know of), the consolation for loss and death has been the belief that there is more to come. Belief in an afterlife, be it another place or another chance, arrives to distract the mourning from their tears.

Because the mourned are in a better place now. Perhaps they are reunited with the other dead. For some they have joined the ancestors, in the never-ending extended family gathering in the sky.

But increasingly, including for those who believe that there is another world beyond this mortal one, peace in the face of death depends on ease with the choices made in life.

Of course, our challenge is to understand what the best choices might be. Without doctrinal guidelines, the quest to live a good life is an unending puzzle. The faithful might find some guidance around which they can shape their lives, but even for them, the question of whether theirs has been a life well lived can be flooring.

By what possible measure can we decide if we have lived our life well?

The number of people touched? Good deeds accomplished? Cruelties avoided?

Treading lightly and trying to do no harm? Saving the planet? Fomenting the revolution?

Getting some laughs? Wiping away a tear (perhaps while offering a plaster and a 'there, there')? Getting up and carrying on when it seems that every effort is meaningless and more exhausting than any body can bear?

Following the rules? Breaking the rules? Being true to yourself? Being of service? Being a character? Being a mensch? Being a respected comrade? Being someone's one true love?

Being?

The grief we feel for our own lives, of course, is something that can only occur with an awareness of our mortality and finitude, and it is the other side of the quest to achieve a life well lived. At its very worst, the fear of missing out, the grief for your own lost life, can freeze. There is such a thin line between giving thanks for the small things and being filled with anxiety that every small thing is not quite good enough. Not quite filled with joy, not lit to best effect. Not quite a moment.

The quest for serenity undergirds the history of human thought, which indicates just how elusive serenity can be. The price that humanity pays for our overdeveloped consciousness—of self, of mortality, of risk and of possibility—is a whole species' existence on high alert. We, more than any other animal, are able to imagine what might come next, what might have been and what we wish might be. The adventure and the challenge of living with this heightened consciousness, probably the thing that Western philosophy has thought of as our humanity, is also a constant negotiation of lives lived with knowledge of grief.

The secular religions of self-help, self-care and self-improvement are devised to meet this horror. The central tenet of each circles around regret and the avoidance of regret, all of which could be summarised as an injunction against mourning your own life. At the same time, the differently constituted anxiety of the age of social media pushes home the uncomfortable knowledge that none of us can in fact do it all, and also that however much we are doing, it will all come to an end.

Living a life well lived must surely include coming to an acceptance of your own finitude. Including an acceptance of what cannot be and what cannot be done. Of the time that there will not be to fill. Of the countless paths that can never be taken. Serenity must include an ability to register the ever-spiralling possibilities and snippets of other not-yet-imagined lives and to be at ease in our connectedness to what others have been and done but that we will never do ourselves.

I wonder, again, if spiritual and political and social and imaginative practices of all kinds circle back to our quest to be serene in the face of mortality. While also hoping to live forever—because this, after all, is the solace promised by the collective subject. You will never miss out because you are part of all these others. Your chapter may end, but the collected chapters will spin out endlessly into the future. You fear that every effort has been meaningless, but it touches so many others that we can never calculate the impact of our lives, and that impossibility of calculation is a retort to finitude.

For all the talk about reconciliation and attending to the past, increasingly I wonder what can possibly be said to give due regard to the millions of unnecessary premature deaths. A plaque here, a speech there and the inevitable calculation. Calculations of different atrocities in the currencies of statistics and of apology. How much suffering merits how much ritual? And what if those who somehow scrabble away from death in these moments prefer not to look back? For them, to memorialise is to leave the wound open, including making apparent the open wound of being a survivor. Accounts of the experiences of Jewish refugees and the aftermath of the Holocaust suggest that people went to considerable lengths not to hear of their experiences. Rather than try again and again to convey unimaginable horror to those wilfully choosing to turn away, perhaps they too decided that survival demanded a pretence of forgetting.

We are accustomed, to an extent, to imagining some forms of racist consciousness as melancholic. The ambivalence of melancholia, desiring simultaneously to absorb and expel its object, runs so close to the strange contradictions of racism. They hate us but they want us. They want to destroy us but also to be us. The racist gaze combines disgust and fascination seamlessly. As a history and a structure, racism must constantly straddle these two strands, rendering people at once expendable and irresistible. Usually, when we speak of racial melancholia, we are referring to the irresolvable ambivalence at the heart of racist domination.

What if we also thought of the experiences of the racially subordinated as giving rise to something like grief?

'Talking about racial grief,' writes Anne Anlin Cheng, 'runs the risk of repeating a tool of containment historically exercised by authority.'[4]

Freud presents melancholia as a kind of mismanaged grief. Fail to process grief in a manner that allows re-entry to the social, and you become stuck in the strange fantasies and pathologies of melancholia. As we see from the seemingly endless stream of post-imperial melancholic behaviours, this stuff can make you do some pretty stupid things.

The racial melancholia of the subordinated is not quite this, or it need not be. The ongoing sorrow born of racialised unbelonging, where the lost object is the fantasy of the self incorporated into the larger whole of a nation or community, is not quite parallel to the ongoing sorrow born of the loss of fantastical racialised privilege. Whereas the second is an irresolvable grief for a racial supremacy that never existed, the first is a sadness that could be resolved if only racial justice were achieved.

---

4 Anne Anlin Cheng, *The Melancholy of Race: Psychoanalysis, Assimilation and Hidden Grief*, New York: Oxford University Press, 2001, p. 14.

The racial melancholia of the subordinated should not be misunderstood as a longing for assimilation or for whiteness, although both these uncomfortable desires are in there somewhere as well. As with so many forms of grief, there are contradictory impulses and irrational longings mixed into the different longing for collective redemption. Experiencing racism does not make us into saints. We, too, catch the glamour of domination and imagine ourselves as made whole in fantasies of subordinating others. We, too, can love the very thing that hates us and tear ourselves apart in the impossible quest to come closer to our love object.

Despite all this, the racial melancholia of the subordinated is not a misrecognition or an inability to process loss as it should be processed. It is the expression of a different hope for what we can be to each other. And in this, perhaps it is not melancholia but heartbreak.

ACCEPTANCE

The apparent normalcy can fool you here. To the inattentive, it can look as if everything is back to normal. Breathe a sigh of relief. No more treading on eggshells. No more having to think hard before you speak. At last, they have fixed themselves up. Thank goodness we won't have to think about that horror any more.

Well, maybe.

I think acceptance is the word for all the people who have learned to keep moving through the world while carrying their wounds. There is no particular heroism or villainy in this. It is just dumb luck, the haphazard distribution of those who can keep going and those who grind to a halt. But, as far as I can see, whatever it is, it is rarely serenity. People tread gingerly but somehow keep on treading. Twist themselves around to protect their weakest spot. Maybe build up something else, some extreme bodily endeavour or ritual of service or quest for pleasure that can disguise the carefully tended wound. This is heartbreak held with care, accommodated into life from then onwards. Sometimes it is a way of learning that heartbreak also has its place.

HISTORY, OR A STORY ABOUT ACCEPTANCE

In *Angels with Dirty Faces*, James Cagney plays one of his most famous roles, laying the ground for the depiction of screen gangsters for the best part of the following century. Cagney is the street kid made good, ruthless and powerful, a famous hardman in his neighbourhood, revered by the local kids, who see themselves in him. When he is caught, convicted and sentenced to death by electrocution, Cagney's character takes pleasure in the continued adulation. The kids are relying on him to be a hardman to the end, to laugh in the face of death. As long as that happens, he can still be their hero.

But in his final meeting with his old friend who has become a priest, Cagney is asked to give up his place in the fantasies and affections of these children. As long as the kids can claim that their man would never be a chicken, they remain in thrall to the fantasy of gangsterism. Cagney is bullish, of course. They are right—he would never be a chicken.

It takes a little time for Cagney to understand what is being asked of him. And it is a big ask. To break the dreams and love of young people whose life-courses are not yet decided. Cagney refuses. He won't do it. He is no chicken.

And then, in the final scene, we see his shadow being dragged screaming and pleading to the chair. And that is what the kids and everyone remembers of him.

I have thought about this way of telling a life story over the years. The test of a good life as a giving up of your place in history.

There is a heretical gospel about Judas Iscariot that recounts a similar tale. Judas is granted insight into the central transformative narrative of Christianity, the one which drags Jesus into the realm of divinity. He has a 'revelation'—or a visit, or a moment of terrible insight into how the world works. And in this moment of clarity, Judas is made to understand that only through his apparent betrayal can the story arc of Christianity be set in play. Without betrayal and capture, there is no crucifixion and resurrection. In the lost Gospel of Judas, it is Jesus himself who gives the instruction: 'for you will sacrifice the man that clothes me.'

Judas grapples with what is being asked. He understands the gravity of the responsibility but also the consequences. To lose your place in history. To have your name become a synonym for weakness and betrayal.

Of course, in the end, he takes the role and exits the narrative.

Why me?

I know this is what we think people say when tragedy hits. Why me? Why us? Why now?

But maybe better to think, why not me? Why not us? Why not now?

There is nothing at all exceptional about grief. Nothing unexpected, really. If you have not been hit yet, we all know it is only a matter of time.

So I wonder what might become possible if we come to see grief as part of our shared humanness and a thing that probably cannot be avoided.

A friend says to me that I must be traumatised by the events of my life. We are close in age and have both weathered some of the all-too-predictable horrors of mid-life and near-death.

I say that everyone is traumatised, apart from those we have known who died young, and sometimes them too. It seems the only two options are to die young or to live with trauma.

Only partly facetiously, I say I prefer the option of living with trauma.

The acceptance of heartbrokenness in our immediate lives signals a will to carry on despite being broken. It is a coming to terms with what cannot be changed (a key phrase in the lexicon of coping with grief). It is not, however, a critique of how sorrow is caused needlessly or a politics that seeks to lessen or end sorrow. When heartbreak arises in response to the avoidable ugliness of this world, acceptance is in danger of running close to quietism.

The account offered by Kübler-Ross is both more and less stark than this. Her interest was in understanding the process of coming to terms with the diagnosis of terminal illness. Acceptance in this context indicated an ability to carry on, to recognise and absorb the implications of the diagnosis, to get one's affairs in order, to cease to be frozen by the spectre of your own death. It is the ability to understand and acknowledge what is happening and then to be able to act in accordance with this knowledge. In the face of our own deaths (which are, after all, inevitable), the ability to remain in the world and to be with others is a form of peace. But this is not an acceptance of the inevitability of suffering or of injustice or of cruelty. The acceptance of mortality requires none of this parking of rage.

There is something in our capacity to grieve that illuminates suffering and unnecessary pain, something in our ability to anticipate death and loss and to imagine what these things feel like, even before we feel them directly, that makes a collective imagination of liberation possible. This is a little more than suggesting that liberation and the will to be liberated are also about empathy. Yes, we do need an affective connection to each other. Perhaps an only imagined affective relation, something like the imagined community of nationhood transposed into dreams of new worlds beyond nations. New ways of marking our kinship and interconnectedness as a shared resource even when the connections remain largely imagined for now. The capacity to grieve opens us to the possibility of imagining collective and diverse pains and, through that, also to comprehend something of the immense diverse and variegated violences that waste our joys and our potentials.

None of this is a kicking against mortality. Wanting to be free is not at all the same as wanting to live forever. As others have said, the cutting desire is to ensure that we all do live before the time runs out.

I say all this as a reminder to myself as much as to anyone else. Trying to numb the pain or to distract ourselves or to leave no room for heartbreak to be spoken because other, far more urgent matters must be attended to, all of that depletes political imagination.

Knowing this does not mean that we should recentre our politics around what is most painful. Neither should we replace our models of organising with therapy. People may need all kinds of things, and perhaps our movements should strive to provide them, but what we do for survival is probably not the same as what we do for change.

I don't think we can become comfortable with heartbrokenness. There is a danger, isn't there, that even the attempt to sit with heartbreak becomes a version of a coping mechanism, of quieting, a way of not being heartbroken after all. We might think of some religious approaches as taking this route of seeking to learn to live with heartbreak almost as a badge of honour. Certainly not as an investigation to remake the mortal world. But for us, salvation must be sought in the realm of the mortal. For those of us dreaming and hoping and scheming for a better world, heartbreak must have its place. We cannot afford to sideline grief, both the grief of human loss and the heartbreak of wasted or painful or disrespected lives. Somehow, we must both resist the push to manage and fix heartbreak and also make a politics that seeks to render heartbreak a thing of the past. Heartbrokenness might be seen as the complex grief of a broken world, necessarily resistant to therapeutic interventions because there is no reasonable response to what we know of the world other than heartbreak.

I was a little worried when I started this piece about the pressure to be upbeat. That is what everyone wants, isn't it? To hear from those who have passed through the abyss and feel that we can all make it out to the other side? No more than another extreme experience to recount with relief, abseiling of the soul. I understand completely that this is why misery memoirs sell. Alongside the undeniable voyeurism—*poke your wounds for us again, go on*—there is a reassurance in hearing survivor stories. Who among us does not fear that they will not survive this?

But sharing heroic stories of resilience is not what I mean when I say heartbrokenness is the class consciousness of racial capitalism. Class consciousness only deserves the name if it goes towards the formation of class agents, even in embryonic form, even when messily intertwined with ways of feeling that are still far from anything we might recognise as 'agency'. The class consciousness of the 'productive class', the proletariat as understood in more orthodox accounts, arises through a combination of understanding of their material position, of the collective nature of this experience and the common cause of workers that arises from this collective experience, and a coming together of the affective investment in self and in collective. It cannot be constituted by sympathy alone, although something like a mutual class sympathy (or 'love') is in play.

The account of racial capitalism unsettles bounded accounts of the proletariat, re-opening the question of who and where (and how) the revolutionary class subject might be. At the very least, and this is no small ask, an attempt to understand racial capitalism must move beyond thinking of accumulation as reliant primarily on the wage relation and instead comprehend a world where capital steals value through a range of methods, including the highly variable processes of expropriation/thievery. People of many kinds suffer, but in very different ways and in a manner that makes it hard to comprehend the links between their material position and that of apparently very different others. Racial capitalism operates, in part, by making us unknowable to each other.

To be anything close to the class consciousness of racial capitalism, heartbreak must be understood as more than an affective state. The heartbreak we are trying to grasp and live with is one that includes elements of analytic understanding, even if only half-articulated, a way of being that registers something of the root of our distinct but connected pains. Perhaps it is also a sense of affinity in suffering—again, a form of love and also a form of sorrow. What is lacking is the appreciation of what might constitute collective agency in this highly variegated context.

I want to suggest that this moment when we begin to see each other, to feel our shared pains in ways that can span locations and terminologies, signals something in this moment of capitalist history. What can be said and felt indicates an opening of possibility, and it is worth some of our energy seeking to understand what. We may not yet have a way to theorise or to organise what a revolutionary anti-capitalist agency might be for our varied pains, but something is opening in the manner in which we can speak our differently located heartbreak.

None of this means we will feel better.

And it is important to say to each other, even as we organise and analyse and struggle and fail, it is all right to feel sad.

WE, THE HEARTBROKEN (OUTRO)

Heartbreak is at the heart of all revolutionary consciousness. How can it not be? Who can imagine another world unless they already have been broken apart by the world we are in?

The heartbreak ripples along underneath and beside the other less dramatic business of political life. A meeting here, a picket there. Something to draft, something to collect, something to deliver. A statement to sign, a hand to hold. Speeches. And more speeches. And still more speeches. A falling out. An election. A split (or two or three) and the odd mourning of denouncing former comrades. And, of course, some more speeches.

But alongside all of that, the relentless busyness that buoys us along, there is always heartbreak. Perhaps we all know that this is the thing we are running from, the thing that must not be said, lest we all break apart completely. No-one devotes the time and the energies and the sheer bloodymindedness that we do unless running from something.

I am calling this something heartbreak because I feel the ache in my chest and the sense of standing at the edge of an abyss and the loss upon loss of the truly heartbroken. And when I feel it, the grief of my own life, the small but devastating losses of any life, the terrible costs of our humanness—all of that ripples out to join the oceans of grief of others. Some others might think of this as a form, a more expansive form, of class consciousness. Let me suggest, only in part to annoy, that to be heartbroken is the true class consciousness of racial capitalism.

Heartbreak is the moment when we see our pain as only a moment in the battle between the will to live and love and the will to destroy.

Heartbreak is when we commune with those who have been broken apart by state violence and we understand that this violence is also meant for us.

Heartbreak is when we realise that there is no remedy, no repair, no way back and nothing to fix this. That whatever comes next these histories and presents of violence cannot be put right. That the destiny of the heartbroken is to wish something better and completely new for those who come next.

Because it is only we, the heartbroken, who can truly battle and long for a world where no-one ever feels like this again.

The jouissance of solidarity

The broken-heartedness of revolutionary consciousness requires a redirection towards the collective. Perhaps some gather here in search of solace. Others simply for distraction. Others still looking for meaning, for a new quest, for something to cancel out their sense of lack. What they have in common is the understanding, often barely articulated, that pain must be turned outwards. That survival, if possible at all, must be in togetherness. Of course, people also guard themselves as they can or must. We also move in and out of the spaces of self-medication, anger and despair. Fall in and out of love and bed with the wrong people. Push away those who nourish, pull close those who harm. Mess things up again and again, but still somehow get up to try once more.

But, at the same time, broken-heartedness thins our skins so we become open to others. The boundaries between us can seem to dissolve, just momentarily. Your pain becomes my pain becomes our pain and the extent of us and the pains we are carrying and the long long way back and the traces across oceans, across centuries, across my street and across your kitchen, all of it overwhelms. I'm awash with it all and I can't remember me. Too too late to find myself, because I have already merged into all of you.

And in a version of the most ancient of stories, the rush into a kind of oblivion leads to a form of ecstasy. In its best everyday forms, the drudgery of political work becomes a falling in love and we are, once again, entranced by each other. Sometimes we reach a little further, enraptured by the jouissance of losing ourselves. Who we were—which identity or which faction, which analysis or which mis/gendering, which skin, which god, which acronym—fades away in the face of who we could be together. And then together doesn't even make sense any more, because in the world we are dreaming and making, there is no me and you, there is only us. Just us forever. And it feels like nothing on earth. Nothing on earth yet.